THE TOP TEN
BATTLES
THAT CHANGED THE WORLD

Chris Oxlade

PowerKiDS
press

New York

Published in 2010 by The Rosen Publishing Group, Inc.
29 East 21st Street, New York 10010

Designed and produced by
David West Books

Designer: Gary Jeffrey
Illustrator: David West
Editor: Katharine Pethick
U.S. Editor: Kara Murray

Photographic credits: 7tl, 8 rosemanios; 7l, Tilemahos Efthimiadis; 23ml, Bundesarchiv; 24l, bernardoh

Library of Congress Cataloging-in-Publication Data

Oxlade, Chris.
The top ten battles that changed the world / Chris Oxlade.
p. cm. — (Top ten)
Includes index.
ISBN 978-1-4358-9176-0 (library binding) — ISBN 978-1-4358-9177-7 (pbk.) —
ISBN 978-1-4358-9178-4 (6-pack)
1. Battles—Juvenile literature. 2. Military history—Juvenile literature. I. Title.
D25.O95 2010
355.4'8—dc22

2009021302

Printed in China

Contents

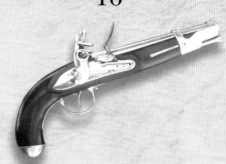

Introduction

The following battles have been selected as the top ten from thousands of battles that have changed our world. Why have these ten made it and not others?

✱ First, it must be a single battle and not a larger military campaign or war.

✱ Second, the battle somehow has to have affected a large part of the world, rather than just one country.

The D-day invasion of 1944 during World War II changed the world, but it consisted of many different battles.

Hannibal's victory over the Romans at Cannae in 216 BC (shown here on a sixteenth-century shield) is a famous battle, but it did not change the world.

The consequences of the Norman victory at the Battle of Hastings in 1066 were important for English history, but they don't directly affect the modern world.

✳ Third, the consequences of the outcome of the battle must have shaped or influenced the world we live in today.

You might disagree with the battles that have been chosen here. In that case, you might want to put together your own list.

Thermopylae

In the spring of 480 BC, the Persians set out to invade Greece, and so expand their powerful empire. At the time, Greece was made up of city-states, such as Athens and Sparta. Sparta was home of the Spartans, the toughest Greek soldiers. Many city-states joined forces and planned to stop the Persians at the narrow pass of Thermopylae. Greatly outnumbered, the Greeks used the confined space in the pass to help fight off the Persians for two days. On the third day, some of the Persian troops, led by a Greek deserter, went around a mountain pass behind Greek lines. Most of the Greeks retreated, but one group, led by 300 Spartans, stayed behind. They fought off wave after wave of Persian attackers, but eventually all of them were killed.

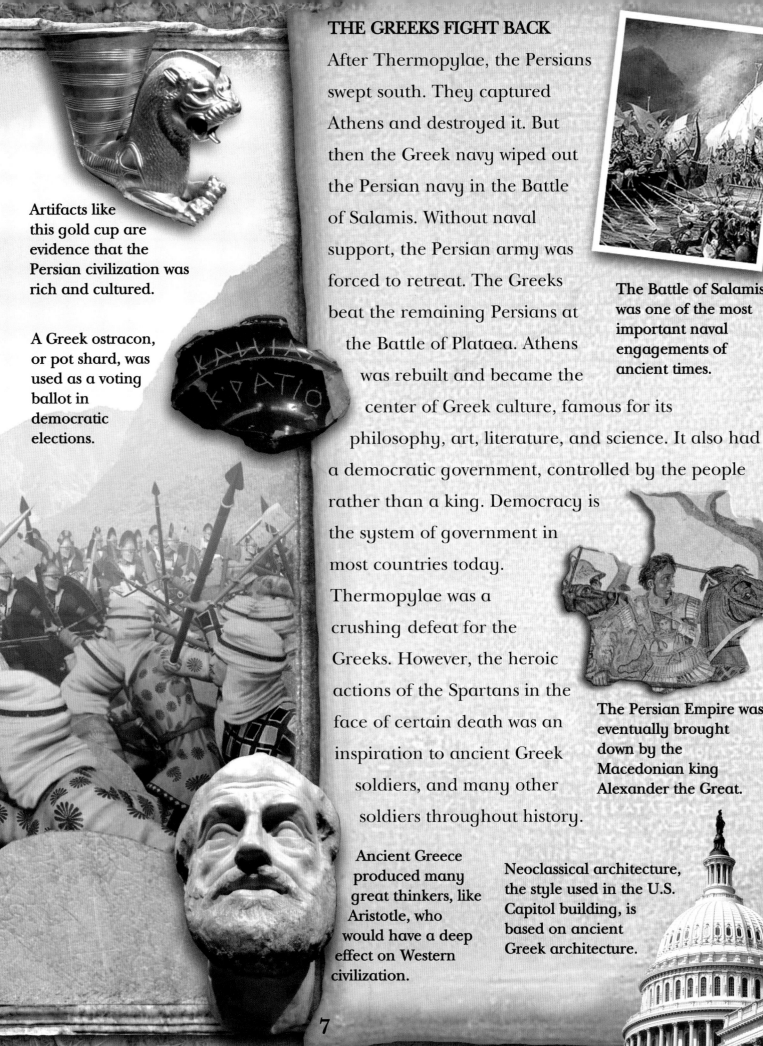

Artifacts like this gold cup are evidence that the Persian civilization was rich and cultured.

A Greek ostracon, or pot shard, was used as a voting ballot in democratic elections.

THE GREEKS FIGHT BACK

After Thermopylae, the Persians swept south. They captured Athens and destroyed it. But then the Greek navy wiped out the Persian navy in the Battle of Salamis. Without naval support, the Persian army was forced to retreat. The Greeks beat the remaining Persians at the Battle of Plataea. Athens was rebuilt and became the center of Greek culture, famous for its philosophy, art, literature, and science. It also had a democratic government, controlled by the people rather than a king. Democracy is the system of government in most countries today. Thermopylae was a crushing defeat for the Greeks. However, the heroic actions of the Spartans in the face of certain death was an inspiration to ancient Greek soldiers, and many other soldiers throughout history.

The Battle of Salamis was one of the most important naval engagements of ancient times.

The Persian Empire was eventually brought down by the Macedonian king Alexander the Great.

Ancient Greece produced many great thinkers, like Aristotle, who would have a deep effect on Western civilization.

Neoclassical architecture, the style used in the U.S. Capitol building, is based on ancient Greek architecture.

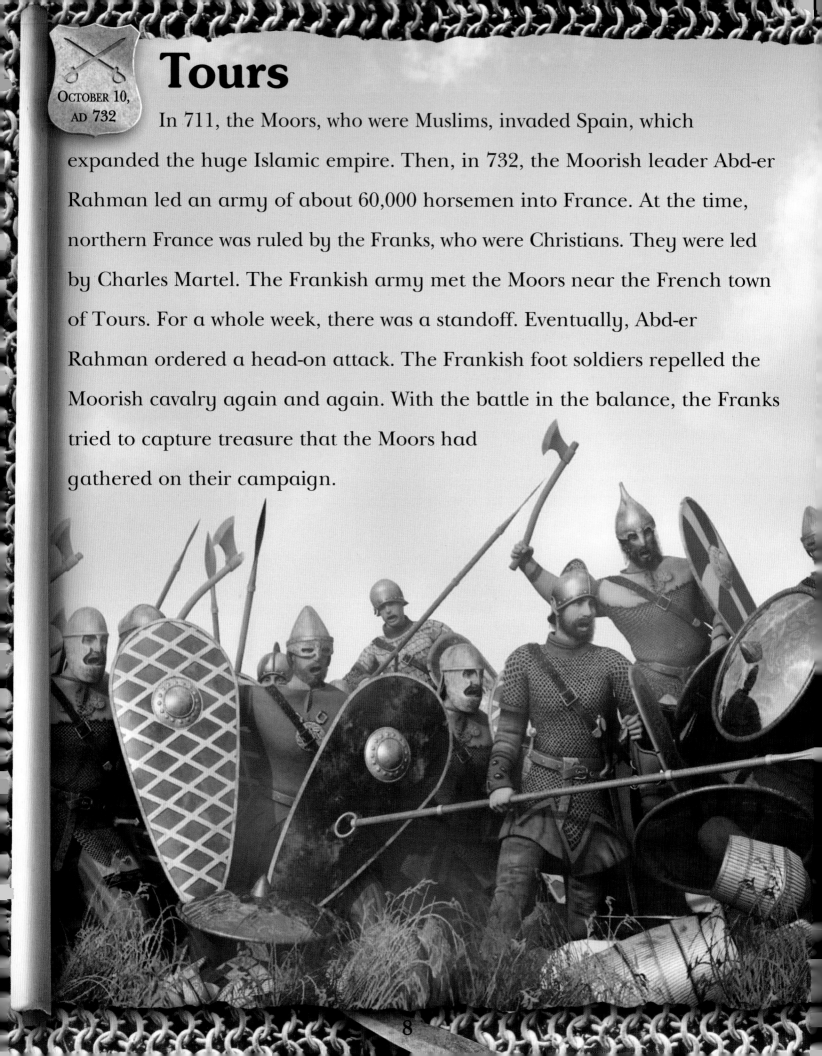

Tours

In 711, the Moors, who were Muslims, invaded Spain, which expanded the huge Islamic empire. Then, in 732, the Moorish leader Abd-er Rahman led an army of about 60,000 horsemen into France. At the time, northern France was ruled by the Franks, who were Christians. They were led by Charles Martel. The Frankish army met the Moors near the French town of Tours. For a whole week, there was a standoff. Eventually, Abd-er Rahman ordered a head-on attack. The Frankish foot soldiers repelled the Moorish cavalry again and again. With the battle in the balance, the Franks tried to capture treasure that the Moors had gathered on their campaign.

Some Moors tried to defend the treasure, but others started to flee the battle. Abd-er Rahman was killed in the confusion. Badly beaten, the Moors retreated during the night.

A TURNING POINT

After Tours, the Franks pushed the Moors back into Spain. Tours remained the farthest point in western Europe ever reached by the Islamic empire. The clash between Christians and Muslims reached its height during the Crusades in the twelfth and thirteenth centuries. Then, Christians tried to capture the part of the Middle East that Christians call the "Holy Land." Modern historians disagree about the importance of the Battle of Tours. Some argue that it preserved the Christian religion and ended a period of expansion for the Islamic empire. Others argue that the Moors were simply after treasure and never intended an invasion. Whichever is the case, Tours was a turning point in the advance of the Islamic empire, halting its spread and changing the world forever.

The Islamic world was scientifically more advanced than the West in the eighth century. The Arab Geber (above) was the first practical alchemist.

The Franks' success allowed feudalism (above) to become the main social system in western Europe.

Charles Martel, whose tomb is seen below, led the Franks to victory in many battles against the invading Muslim forces (right).

Lepanto

In 1571, two fleets of galleys faced each other near the port of Lepanto, in western Greece. One fleet, of 206 galleys and six galleasses, or larger armed ships, belonged to the Holy League. The other, slightly larger, fleet belonged to the Ottoman Turks. The Ottomans boasted a vast empire, and their navy controlled the Mediterranean Sea.

The Holy League was formed in 1570 to oppose the Ottomans. It included Spain, Venice, Genoa, and the Papal States of Italy. The battle started badly for the Ottomans as they lost galleys to the powerful Holy League galleasses.

In the middle of the battle, the two flagships met. The Turkish ship was boarded and their leader, Ali Pasha, was killed. The surviving Turks withdrew. The Holy League had won the battle in just three hours.

The Ottoman armies had managed to attack Vienna in Austria by 1529.

THE OTTOMAN DECLINE

During the battle, the Ottoman fleet lost nearly all its galleys. Many were sunk, but most were captured. The Turks suffered 25,000 dead and wounded and also lost about 10,000 Christian galley slaves. The Holy League lost 50 galleys and had 13,000 dead and wounded, but it gained control of the Mediterranean waters. The Turks rebuilt their fleet of galleys, but they could not quickly replace the highly trained sailors and troops they had lost. The Holy League's victory at Lepanto stopped the Ottoman Empire's advance into Europe. It probably saved Rome, the home of the Pope, from invasion. Within a few decades, the powerful Ottoman Empire was in decline. Lepanto showed that the Ottman Turks could be defeated. It was a real turning point in history.

The Holy League ships fielded harquebusiers, fighters who were armed with an early type of gun, called a matchlock.

The battle held huge religious significance for the Roman Catholic world.

The city of Venice, Italy, was a member of the Holy League.

Poltava

In the seventeenth century, Sweden was the most powerful country in northern Europe, with an empire that stretched into present-day Poland and Russia. Peter the Great, the czar of Russia, wanted to control the Baltic Sea. He unsuccessfully attacked Sweden in 1700, thereby starting the Great Northern War. In 1708, the Swedish army, led by their king, Charles XII, moved farther into Russia. But the harsh winter, constant Russian raids, and disease left them severely weakened, with only about 14,000 healthy fighting men. In 1709, the Swedes attacked the fort at Poltava, near Kiev, which was defended by about 45,000 Russians. The Swedish infantry advance floundered because their cavalry support arrived too late to help them. Charles ordered his army to retreat. The Russians were victorious.

A wounded Charles XII with Cossack leader Mazepa sees his army defeated.

RISE OF THE RUSSIAN EMPIRE

After the battle, Charles XII fled to Turkey. He returned to Sweden five years later, but it was too late. As Sweden became weaker, Russia became stronger. After Poltava, Peter the Great moved his capital from Moscow to St. Petersburg, the Baltic port he had always wanted. He expanded Russia with military victories over other nearby countries and turned his country from a poor agricultural nation into a major power in northern Europe, which it remains to this day. The Battle of Poltava shifted the balance of power in Europe from Sweden to Russia, making it a hugely important battle.

Swedish monarch Charles XII (right) wanted to equal the conquests of the founder of the Swedish empire, Gustavus Adolphus (above).

One of Russia's Northern War gains became its new capital, St. Petersburg, in 1703.

Peter the Great transformed the Czardom of Russsia into a great empire.

The Russian Empire eventually collapsed in a series of dramatic revolutions starting in 1905.

Saratoga

The American Revolution began in 1775, with fighting between American colonists and British forces. In 1777, an army of British soldiers, under the command of General John Burgoyne, marched south from Canada, aiming to join up with British forces in New York City. The Americans, led by General Horatio Gates, formed a defensive position overlooking the Hudson River near the hamlet of Saratoga. Two battles followed, together called the Battle of Saratoga. Burgoyne tried to bypass the Americans. However, he was cut off at the Battle of Freeman's Farm. The British captured the farm but suffered heavy losses. Burgoyne then waited for reinforcements to arrive from New York City. They never came.

Fierce fighting at the Battle of Bemis Heights followed 18 days later. Burgoyne's attack was unsuccessful. The British had to retreat.

Horatio Gates, a British soldier who became an American general, was the victor at Saratoga.

BEGINNING OF THE END FOR BRITAIN

The British fled to Saratoga, where they were surrounded and forced to surrender. With the capture of an entire British army, the Americans now had control of the northern American states. The French saw that the Americans had a chance of winning the war and declared war on Britain the next year. This forced Britain to abandon its fight in the north, and its armies concentrated on the southern states instead. The British were finally defeated in 1781 and forced out of America for good. Most historians agree that Saratoga was the decisive battle in America's struggle for independence from Britain, enabling it to grow from a colony into a major power that would change the world.

After the American victory at Saratoga, the French navy joined the fight against the British.

British commander Lord Cornwallis surrendered to French and American troops at Yorktown in 1781.

The Battle of Saratoga is commemorated by this monument on the site of the battlefield.

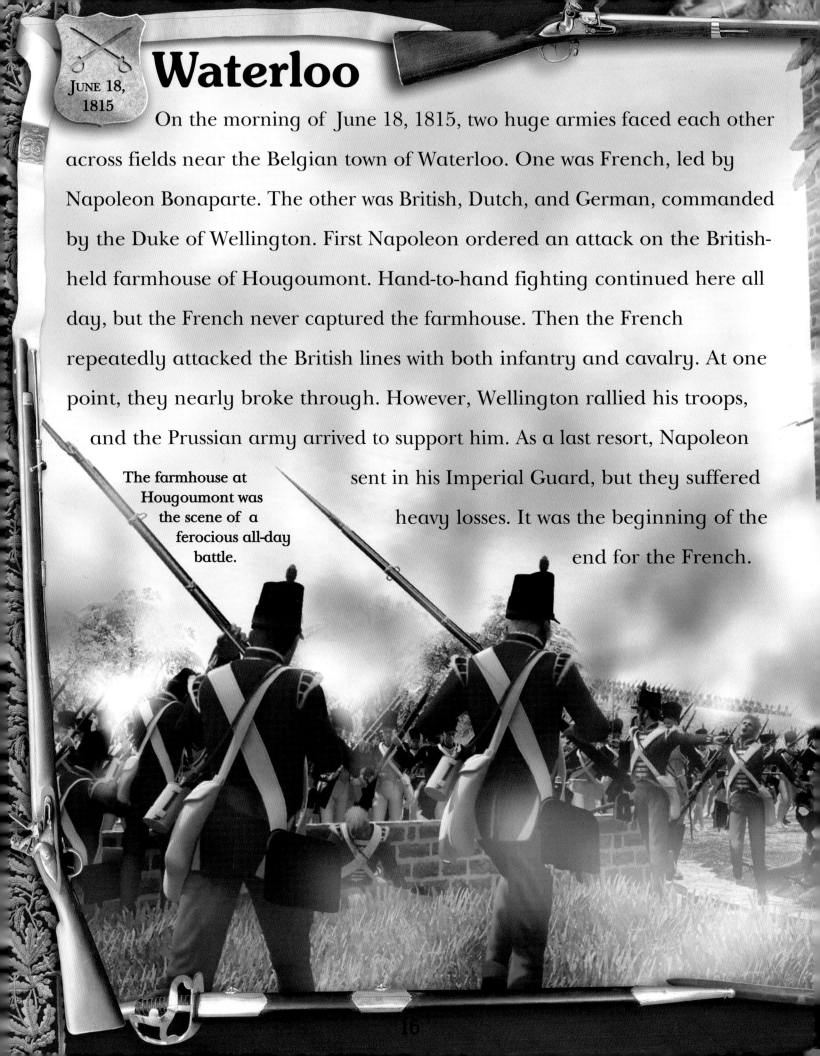

Waterloo

On the morning of June 18, 1815, two huge armies faced each other across fields near the Belgian town of Waterloo. One was French, led by Napoleon Bonaparte. The other was British, Dutch, and German, commanded by the Duke of Wellington. First Napoleon ordered an attack on the British-held farmhouse of Hougoumont. Hand-to-hand fighting continued here all day, but the French never captured the farmhouse. Then the French repeatedly attacked the British lines with both infantry and cavalry. At one point, they nearly broke through. However, Wellington rallied his troops, and the Prussian army arrived to support him. As a last resort, Napoleon sent in his Imperial Guard, but they suffered heavy losses. It was the beginning of the end for the French.

The farmhouse at Hougoumont was the scene of a ferocious all-day battle.

NAPOLEON EXILED

Waterloo was the last battle of the Napoleonic Wars, during which Napoleon Bonaparte, the French emperor, built up a powerful empire. The empire began to collapse in 1812, when Napoleon was forced to retreat from Spain and Russia. Napoleon was exiled in 1814, but returned to power in 1815. In response, Britain, Austria, and Prussia, among others, decided to join forces and invade France. They were assembling their armies in Belgium when Napoleon tried to stop them at Waterloo. After the battle, Napoleon escaped but later surrendered. He was exiled to the island of St. Helena, where he died in 1821. The Battle of Waterloo ended French domination of western Europe and helped Europe stay peaceful for 35 years.

47,000 soldiers were killed or injured fighting at Waterloo.

Wellington went on to become one of Britain's most distinguished statesmen.

Famous for Napoleon's defeat, "Waterloo" came to mean "a terrible downfall" or "a crushing loss."

The next major European conflict would be the Crimean War in the 1850s.

17

Gettysburg

After the election of Abraham Lincoln in 1860, 11 Southern states broke away from the United States. They were afraid that after Lincoln became president, he would end the practice of slavery. The Southern states formed the Confederacy, and those in the North remaining loyal to the federal government were called the Union. They went to war in 1861, beginning the Civil War. In 1863, Confederate and Union forces met at Gettysburg, Pennsylvania. In the first day of the battle, the Confederates won a series of skirmishes. By the second day, the Union soldiers had organized a defensive line. The Confederates attacked it, but, despite heavy losses, the Union held on. On the third day, 12,500 Confederate soldiers rushed the Union lines. This event is now known as Pickett's Charge, for one of the generals in command. The charge was a disaster, and half the soldiers never returned. The Confederate forces retreated in defeat.

CONFEDERATE HIGH WATER MARK

Abraham Lincoln (1809–1865)

Pickett's Charge was the Confederates' "high-water mark," or the closest they got to winning the war. The defeat ended Confederate general Robert E. Lee's attempt to invade the Northern states. The following months saw two important Union victories. As the armies marched south, General Ulysses S. Grant's army captured Vicksburg, Mississippi, and General William Tecumseh Sherman's captured Atlanta. The war finally ended in 1865 when General Lee, short of men and supplies, surrendered. Five days later, President Abraham Lincoln was shot and killed by a Confederate sympathizer. The Civil War brought the United States together again and ended slavery in the Southern states. Gettysburg was the battle that gave the Union the upper hand in this war, the outcome of which would change the world.

General Grant accepts Lee's surrender in 1865.

The Union army gave a victory parade in Washington, D.C. The Union war effort changed America into a powerful, industrialized nation.

Battle of Britain

"The Battle of France is over. I expect the Battle of Britain is about to begin," said British Prime Minister Winston Churchill in the midst of World War II. By June 1940, the Germans had swept through France. Britain was their next target. Before an invasion could start, the Germans needed to gain control of the skies and that meant destroying Britain's Royal Air Force. During August 1940, the Luftwaffe attacked RAF airfields. The RAF fought back. Each side lost hundreds of aircraft and pilots. By early September, the RAF was close to collapsing. However, the Luftwaffe switched its attacks to London, in response to RAF attacks on German cities. This gave the RAF valuable breathing space. Within weeks, the Luftwaffe was losing so many aircraft that daytime bombing raids were stopped. The Battle of Britain had been won.

THE FEW

After failing to beat the RAF, Hitler postponed his plans to invade Britain. German bombers continued night raids on London and other cities. Tens of thousands of civilians were killed before these raids finally stopped early in 1941. Referring to his pilots, Churchill said, "Never in the field of human conflict was so much owed by so many to so few." The Battle of Britain was Germany's first defeat during World War II, and changed the opinion in the United States that Britain could not survive the German onslaught. It saved Britain from invasion, allowed it to build up its forces, and, later, to be the launchpad for the Allies to retake France in 1944.

RAF fighter aces, like Robert Stanford Tuck, were the heroes who saved their homeland.

London during the Blitz

Winston Churchill gives his famous "V for victory" sign to the British people.

The head of the Luftwaffe, Hermann Göring (left)

The invasion of France was launched from Britain's coasts.

Stalingrad

In June 1941, Germany launched Operation Barbarossa, the invasion of the Soviet Union. A year later, Hitler ordered his Sixth Army to capture Stalingrad, an important industrial city. In response, the Soviet leader, Joseph Stalin, ordered his generals to defend the city at all costs. The Luftwaffe bombed the city into rubble, but the Soviet troops used the ruins as cover and the Germans had to fight against them hand-to-hand. By the end of October, the Germans were nearly exhausted. Then, the Soviets attacked with fresh troops and the Germans were surrounded. Despite air drops, they gradually ran out of ammunition, fuel, and food. The Germans surrendered in January 1943.

Soviet leader Joseph Stalin ordered anyone who could carry a gun to rush to the defense of the city that bore his name.

Hitler needed access to Russian oilfields to fuel the war.

GERMANS IN RETREAT

The Battle of Stalingrad was one of the bloodiest of World War II. The Soviets lost more than 1 million soldiers. At the height of the battle, the life expectancy of a Soviet soldier was just one day. The Germans also lost an entire army. About 200,000 men were dead or injured and 90,000 were taken prisoner, with a vast number of tanks and other equipment destroyed. The remaining German forces in the Soviet Union could not withstand the Soviet advance and, over the next two years, were pushed right back into Germany. The Battle of Stalingrad was the turning point of Operation Barbarossa. It did not end the war itself, but critically weakened Germany, ensuring its defeat. The Soviet Union went on to dominate Eastern Europe for over 40 years.

The cold, the terrain, and the Red Army proved to be too much for the German soldiers.

Hitler didn't want to repeat Napoleon's 1812 retreat from Russia.

The Motherland Calls, one of the tallest statues in the world, commemorates the Battle of Stalingrad.

Soviet forces eventually fought their way to Berlin at the end of the war in 1945.

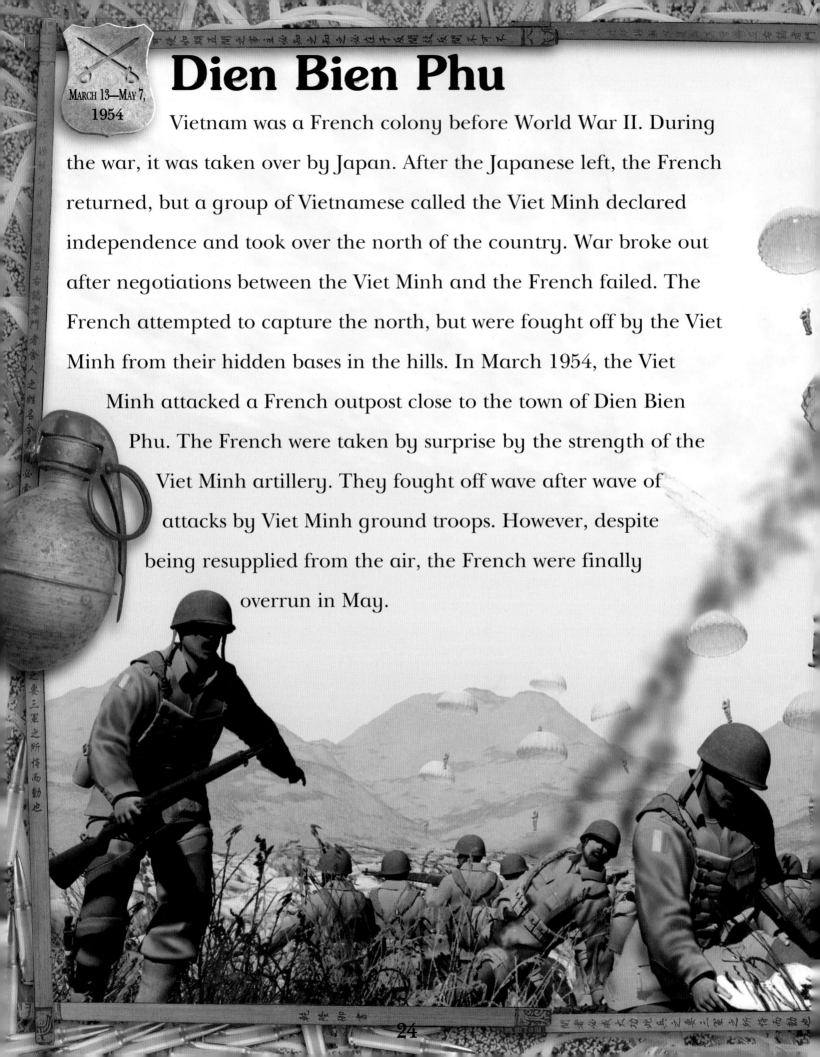

Dien Bien Phu

Vietnam was a French colony before World War II. During the war, it was taken over by Japan. After the Japanese left, the French returned, but a group of Vietnamese called the Viet Minh declared independence and took over the north of the country. War broke out after negotiations between the Viet Minh and the French failed. The French attempted to capture the north, but were fought off by the Viet Minh from their hidden bases in the hills. In March 1954, the Viet Minh attacked a French outpost close to the town of Dien Bien Phu. The French were taken by surprise by the strength of the Viet Minh artillery. They fought off wave after wave of attacks by Viet Minh ground troops. However, despite being resupplied from the air, the French were finally overrun in May.

COLD WAR CONFLICT

The defeat at Dien Bien Phu was a disaster for the French, and they decided to pull out of Vietnam. Vietnam was then split in half, with North Vietnam governed by the Communist Viet Minh and South Vietnam by a non-Communist government. Then war broke out again between the North and South in 1959. China and the Soviet Union supported the North.

Vietnam, a former French colony, was divided into two sections in 1954.

Ho Chi Minh was the North Vietnamese leader.

In 1965, the United States, concerned about the spread of Communism in Asia, sent troops. The American campaign was a disaster, and they withdrew in 1973. The North took control of all of Vietnam in 1975. The Battle of Dien Bien Phu showed that determined fighters with local knowledge could beat a modern military power. The Vietcong fought the Americans in the same way, making Dien Bien Phu a turning point in the way modern conflicts are fought.

U.S. forces withdrew from Vietnam after a disastrous eight-year campaign. The failure of this war influences U.S. foreign policy to this day.

The Best of the Rest

BATTLE OF ACTIUM (31 BC)

The Battle of Actium was fought during a civil war between the rival Roman forces of Octavian and Mark Antony, which raged from 44 BC to 27 BC. On one side of this naval battle were 260 ships led by Marcus Agrippa, fighting for Octavian. On the other were 220 ships belonging to Mark Antony and the Egyptian queen Cleopatra. The battle began when Antony's ships attacked using missile-throwing machines. Agrippa's ships fought back. Only when Cleopatra ordered her ships to withdraw did Agrippa get the upper hand. Most of Antony's ships were sunk. His army was left stranded on shore and surrendered. He and Cleopatra committed suicide. Octavian conquered Egypt and, in 27 BC, became the first Roman emperor (under the name Augustus).

The defeat of Antony and Cleopatra at Actium allowed Octavian to become the first Roman emperor.

BATTLE OF THE TEUTOBURG FOREST (AD 9)

In AD 9, Teutoburg Forest (in modern-day Germany) was at the northern border of the Roman Empire. Publius Quinctilius Varus led three Roman legions, with more than 20,000 men, to stop a rebellion by local tribes. Led by Arminius, a former ally of Varus, a force of over 10,000 men drawn from several Germanic tribes were waiting for them. The Romans were marching in a long column along a muddy forest track. The tribes attacked the column in several places. When the Romans tried to escape the next day, the tribes attacked again. Finally, the Romans marched into a trap set by Arminius and were wiped out. Varus killed himself. The victory of the Germanic tribes at Teutoburg Forest ended the Roman expansion into northern Europe.

Arminius, the hero of Teutoburg

BATTLE OF VIENNA (1683)

In July 1683, the forces of the Turkish Ottoman Empire began a siege of Vienna. The Turks wanted to expand their empire, and Vienna was an important strategic city. However, the troops and citizens, about 17,000 in all, inside the city walls refused to surrender. After two months, the defenders were short on food and ammunition, and the Turks were ready to break into the city. Then, in the nick of time, help arrived in the form of Polish, Austrian, and German troops. The Polish infantry attacked the Turks on the morning of September 12. In the afternoon, 20,000 cavalry also charged the Turks in the largest cavalry charge in history. They broke the Turkish lines and the Turks retreated in panic. The Battle of Vienna was the turning point in the Ottoman-Habsburg wars. It stopped the Ottomans from advancing farther into Europe.

The Siege of Vienna involved enormous numbers of men.

BATTLE OF BLENHEIM (1704)

After the death of King Charles II of Spain in 1700, Britain, Austria, and other nations fought the War of the Spanish Succession (1701–1714) to prevent the French king Louis XIV from gaining control of Spain. In 1704, the French were threatening to capture Vienna. The British and Austrians, led by the British general the Duke of Marlborough, met them at Blenheim, in modern-day Germany. Marlborough's cavalry broke through the French lines and forced many of them into the Danube River. It was a crushing defeat for the French. They lost tens of thousands of men who were killed, wounded, captured, or drowned. The Battle of Blenheim was the first defeat for the French army in 50 years. More victories followed for the Duke of Marlborough and his allies. By 1714, the French were forced to ask for peace.

Part of an eighteenth-century tapestry commemorating the Battle of Blenheim

The Duke of Marlborough